Colors of Loss and Healing

Colors of Loss and Healing

An Adult Coloring Book for Getting Through Tough Times

DEBORAH S. DERMAN, PhD

Illustrations by **LISA POWELL BRAUN**

RODALE.

RODALE
wellness

Live happy. Be healthy. Get inspired.

Sign up today to get exclusive access to our authors, exclusive bonuses,
and the most authoritative, useful, and cutting-edge information on health,
wellness, fitness, and living your life to the fullest.

Visit us online at RodaleWellness.com
Join us at RodaleWellness.com/Join

Portions of this book were previously published in *Colors of Loss and Healing* by CreateSpace Independent
Publishing Platform in 2016.

Rodale books may be purchased for business or promotional use or for special sales. For information, please write to:
Special Markets Department, Rodale, Inc., 733 Third Avenue, New York, NY 10017

Printed in the United States of America

Rodale Inc. makes every effort to use acid-free ♾, recycled paper ♻.

Illustrations by Lisa Powell Braun

Library of Congress Cataloging-in-Publication Data is on file with the publisher.

ISBN 978-1-62336-928-6 paperback

Distributed to the trade by Macmillan

2 4 6 8 10 9 7 5 3 1 paperback

Follow us @RodaleBooks on

We inspire health, healing, happiness, and love in the world.
Starting with you.

Introduction

When I was 27, a dear friend and neighbor knocked on my door to take back his vacuum cleaner. I found out the next day that I was last person he spoke to—he killed himself, using the vacuum hose, shortly after he saw me that night.

Nine years later, I was a happily married mother of a toddler, eager for a visit from my parents. My 16-month-old son and I were at the airport waiting to greet the private plane my father was piloting with my mother and their best friends aboard.

Out of nowhere, the plane fell from the sky and crashed in front of us. All four passengers died. A faulty gas line turned out to be the cause of the malfunction that led to the crash.

Then, almost 4 years later, my husband died suddenly of a heart attack while playing rugby. I was 39 and suddenly widowed with two small children and pregnant with our third child. My parents were gone, and my siblings lived across the country.

Several years after losing my husband, I was diagnosed with a rare form of breast cancer. I had to face my worst fear: would I die and leave my children orphaned?

I know my history sounds almost too terrible to be true. I recall that after each crisis, I was devastated and overwhelmed by unrelenting fear, confusion, and pain. But I remember my sister saying something that has carried me through the hardest of times: "One day this will be your past," she said. She was right, although I did not and could not believe her then.

Over time, I learned how to navigate and survive the many challenges that life threw my way. I survived breast cancer, raised three great kids, married a wonderful man who has become the adoptive father of my children, and found my calling as a grief counselor, even earning a doctorate focused on that area.

I received a coloring book for my last birthday. There were hundreds if not thousands of little spaces to color; the task of finishing even one illustration seemed daunting. I did, however, pick up a pencil and began to fill in the spaces with color. The act of coloring was soothing and calming. After several hours, I had completed a whole page and soon completed the entire book. It suddenly occurred to me that coloring is a beautiful metaphor for progressing through grief and loss. All you have to do is begin somewhere, pick up a pencil, and complete one small space at a time.

My hope is that the good that comes out of my tragedies will be my ability to help others cope with loss. This is why I've created this coloring book.

THE ILLUSTRATIONS

Each page of this book was beautifully illustrated by Lisa Powell Braun. The illustrations are symbolic of things in my own life that have great meaning to me.

The chairs, the windows, the birdhouse, and the perennials are all things that I have in my home and bring me great comfort. The morning glories on the cover are flowers that I plant from seed each spring. These deep blue blossoms live only during the day, but as they die each evening, a new bud sets up for the next morning.

You'll also notice a word embedded within each illustration. The words that I have chosen have been derived from both my personal and professional experiences. These are the things that I think are most important as a person heals from loss. I believe that these words can give you a blueprint toward healing.

The Labrador Retriever in the "family" illustration is a picture of my dog, Teddy. I got him as a puppy when I was healing from breast cancer. He knew he had a job to do, and he did it well. The flowers in the "memory" illustration were planted at my first home. I have replanted these same flowers at my new home with my new husband. "Cherish" is a special word for me as well. My first husband and I would take many walks on the beach and surprise each other with a little shell at the end of our walk. I have kept these shells for 24 years, and they are illustrated here in the book.

As you color, reflect on each word. Use the journaling pages to write your thoughts or draw on your own picture. Think about the images that are personally relevant to you in your own life.

What meaning does each word have for you? What images come to mind?

HOW TO USE THIS BOOK

Clear a space for coloring. Remove the bills, the legal documents, medical records, and mail from the table. They will only serve to distract you. This is your time to be calm and focused. Take a few minutes each day to sit and color. Take as little or as much time as you'd like.

The pages in this book can be colored in any order. As you start to color a page, focus on the page's word. What meaning does that word have for you? Grief is not an orderly affair, and these words can apply at any time in your healing process. "Wisdom," for example, can happen early in a loss, and certainly appears as we go through healing.

Color whatever word or whichever illustration appeals to you at the moment. The right way is your own way. Everyone's journey is different, and your thoughts and feelings will be uniquely yours. Coloring gives you the time, however, to take pause.

This book also has blank pages for your own journaling. Take the time to write down your own words, thoughts, and feelings as you go through each page. What things do you cherish? How do you value family and friends? What small steps are you taking toward healing? No one goes through loss and grieving in exactly the same way. Write. Draw. Experiment with color. It is your journey and your process, and it is unique to you.

Coloring Together

Many times, people will color with friends or families. When people color together, conversation starts to flow. Words that were previously unspoken can now be shared within the safe structure of this book. Communicating thoughts and feelings are incredibly important to the healing process.

Coloring Alone

I cannot count the number of sleepless nights I spent in anguish and sadness many years ago. It seemed that every catastrophic event I could invent became real in the deepest part of the night. Use this book in those moments of despair, and start to color. The meditative process will relax you and each healing word will focus your thoughts. Clarity of thought will guide you as you move forward. Be sure that you use the journaling pages. Writing down your thoughts and feelings can be very therapeutic. Write whatever you want. No one has to see but you.

MY HOPE FOR YOU

As we go through difficult times, we need determination and confidence that we will survive, and survive well. We need good counsel to tell us we can and will live fully again, and we need to make meaning of the challenges that life has brought our way. We need to become deeper, wiser people. What is important to you now? Who is important to you now? What do you want to do with your life that gives you purpose and meaning?

This book can guide you through the healing process by helping you to consider the elements I think are necessary for recovery. Leave the book open on the table, and have your pencils close at hand. All you have to do is color one space at a time...one page at time...one day at a time.

My palette... my words... my thoughts

y palette... my words... my thoughts

My palette... my words... my thoughts

My palette... my words... my thoughts

My palette... my words... my thoughts

My palette... my words... my thoughts

My palette... my words... my thoughts

y palette... my words... my thoughts

My palette... my words... my thoughts

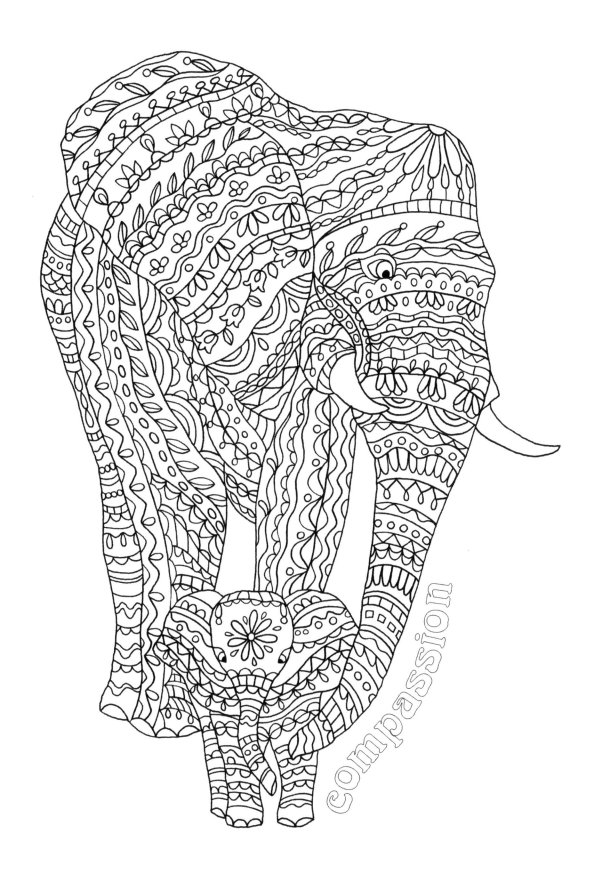

My palette... my words... my thoughts

My palette... my words... my thoughts

My palette... my words... my thoughts

My palette... my words... my thoughts

y palette... my words... my thoughts

My palette... my words... my thoughts

My palette... my words... my thoughts

My palette... my words... my thoughts

y palette... my words... my thoughts

My palette... my words... my thoughts

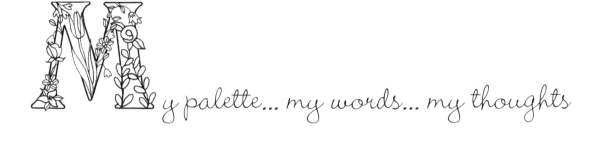

My palette... my words... my thoughts

My palette... my words... my thoughts

 y palette... my words... my thoughts

y palette... my words... my thoughts

y palette... my words... my thoughts

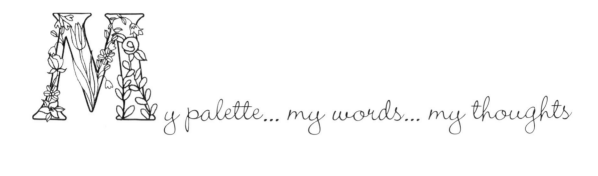

My palette... my words... my thoughts

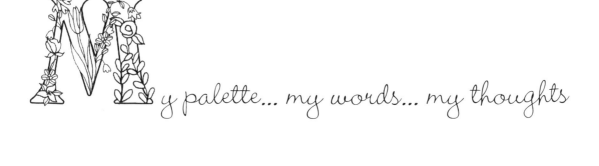

My palette... my words... my thoughts

My palette... my words... my thoughts

y palette... my words... my thoughts

Prioritize

My palette... my words... my thoughts

y palette... my words... my thoughts

My palette... my words... my thoughts

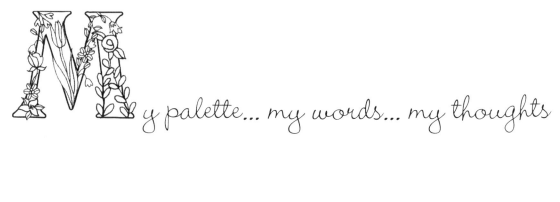

My palette... my words... my thoughts

My palette... my words... my thoughts

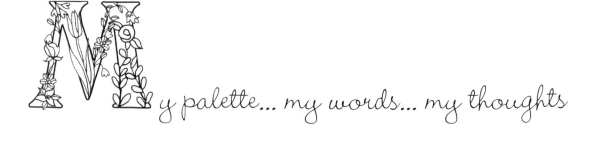

My palette... my words... my thoughts

My palette... my words... my thoughts

My palette... my words... my thoughts

My palette... my words... my thoughts

y palette... my words... my thoughts

y palette... my words... my thoughts

y palette... my words... my thoughts

y palette... my words... my thoughts

My palette... my words... my thoughts

Give Back

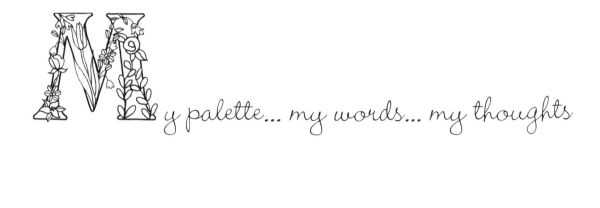

y palette... my words... my thoughts

y palette... my words... my thoughts

About the Author

Deborah S. Derman, PhD, is a grief counselor who lives in Dresher, PA. She has been in private practice for more than 20 years.

Lisa Powell Braun is an artist and illustrator. She also lives in Dresher, PA.